‡RICHER Press

An Imprint of Richer Life, LLC

RICHER Press is a full service, specialty Trade publisher whose sole goal is to *shape thoughts and change lives for the better*. All of the books, eBooks and digital media we publish, distribute and market embrace our commitment to help maximize opportunities for personal growth and professional achievement.

To learn more visit

www.richerlifellc.com.

Take Two Cookies
and Call Me
in the Morning

In loving memory
of my grandmother

Fanny A. Harris

whose wisdom, unconditional acceptance,
and always full cookie jar assisted me
in discovering the main ingredients
in this recipe for "Loving."

Praise for *Take Two Cookies and Call Me in the Morning*

A Story of How to Connect in a Disconnected World

"Nancy understands, embraces, and unfolds the source of our connection to others: the prime directive of a loving God . . . LOVE. She writes in a sensitive, vulnerable, and easy-to-follow style, allowing hurting and disconnected people to find hope in connecting with others and baking their own love-filled Chocolate Chip Cookies. A must read for therapists and their clients."

> — **Rev. David R. Henson, Ph.D.,**
> **Licensed Clinical Pastoral Counselor**

"I am inspired and awed by the power of Nancy's simple cookie approach to counseling. It is more than effective — it is delicious!"

> — **Hilary Shulman, Managing Director,**
> **Intermediary Alliances Munder**
> **Capital Management**

"The principles Nancy uses in her therapies have literally changed my life! Her range of knowledge and the breadth of her abilities is truly astounding! I was thrilled to discover how well she captured them in her simple book. She has searched for the profound and revealed the inner wisdom that we all know in our hearts to be true."

> — **Lynn Inmon, Teacher**

Praise Continued:

"*Take Two Cookies and Call Me in the Morning* successfully takes on the big question of finding the meaning in one's life, and accomplishes it in a very readable and practical manner."

> — Gary J. Hershoren, EdD.,
> Counselor Emeritus (retired)

"*A deceptively simple recipe for a sweeter, more enjoyable, and more productive life. The cookie metaphor makes the information so easy to digest.*"

> — Alan J. Parisse, CSP, CPAE
> Hall of Fame Speaker

"Nancy Harris takes a very complex philosophy and puts it into terms anyone can understand and use. She has a real gift for showing by example and employing life's lessons to deepen your awareness."

> — Michelle L. Sullivan,
> Licensed Massage Therapist

"As I look back on the relationships I have had, this book shows why some worked and some did not. It presents powerful truths in a short, easy-to-read style. I have read it several times and learn more each time."

> — Robert Berman, Senior Systems Manager,
> Human Resources and Training
> TAP Pharmaceutical Products, Inc.

Acknowledgments:

Sometimes events happen in our lives that require us to change directions, take a stand, or fulfill an inner longing or knowing. Sometimes we do not know the "How-To" that is required. Then we find ourselves on an unexpected journey of discovery. Writing this book has taught me that it is not the completion that provides the greatest benefits, but instead the adventure.

The journey that brought me to *Take Two Cookies and Call Me in the Morning* started thirty-three years ago. Throughout those three decades there have been many people who have played very important roles in assisting me in learning about "loving"; to all of you, my deepest and heartfelt thanks.

My love and gratitude goes to everyone who has been directly involved with the creation of this book:

Shannon Parish – Illustrations and Cover Design
CreativeVirtualOffice.com and artbyshannon.com

Karen Saunders Assistance with Interior Layout and Cover, MacGraphics Services: www.macgraphics.net

Laren Bright – Copy Editor, and role model for how to live in the "Loving"

Ted Case – for motivation, computer lessons, encouragement, research assistance, and friendship

Christine Testolini – Publishing Consultant — for helping me through the maze of the publishing world

Karen Tjernlund – for her offhanded comment that became the title of this book and for thirty years of friendship

Paul Richter – Mentor and dear friend, thanks for teaching me so much of what is in this book

Trudy Welty – for helping me realize the depth of my potential and not letting me quit

John-Roger and John Morton – whose spiritual teachings have guided my journey for over fifteen years. Special thanks for helping me realize that there was more than one book for me to write.

Jonathon and Maurissa Morningstar – for your original faith in me and this story. I would not have started writing if you had not passed through my life when you did.

PLUS,
Ann Marie Gordon, David Pasikov, Margaret Griffith, Ilene Harris, my mother Marcia Harris, and Bruce Gibson. And, all my friends and clients that read prototypes, helped with title decisions, and patiently supported me through this process.

Once upon a time, not so terribly long ago, in an era of fairy-tale lives, when TV was a miracle, space exploration was a school-stopping event, plastic was the future, and fear simmered under it all, on a faraway college campus lived a young woman named Liz.

Liz's parents worried about their "strange and unique" daughter, who had always marched to a different drummer. They hoped that college would help her gain skills that would prepare her for a career. They suggested Social Work, Teaching, or Nursing.

But those female-appropriate vocations didn't interest Liz. She wanted to pursue knowledge and wisdom. She quested for the answers to the meaning of life.

She was bound and determined to find the answers to:

"Who am I?"

"Why am I here?"

"What is my Life Purpose?"

"Why do I feel so different from everyone else?"

And most of all…
"What is Love?"

So, she took classes in
    Philosophy,
    Sociology,
    Psychology,
    Political Science,
    Archaeology, and more!!

Liz even tried agriculture and skiing.

She learned many concepts and
gained lots of information.

She could recite compelling statistics and
quote great philosophers.

Yet, the answers to her questions
(which were really about the secret to
happiness and love) eluded her.

Liz's mind and heart struggled with why nations wage war.

The pain of grieving mothers who had lost their sons or daughters troubled her deeply.

The cry of a hungry child and the bigotry and the hypocrisy of people who professed love and forgiveness, but demonstrated otherwise, ripped her to the core.

Her dorm mates and her best friend, Marge, told her that her concerns were really her longing to experience Love and turned the conversations to men and to sex.

Liz decided that maybe they were right. She knew she was supposed to be looking for love.

After all, going to college was about getting a MRS.

Wasn't it?

So, she accepted dates and hoped that love would make her feel whole and normal.

She hoped that love would give her a sense of belonging and purpose, as it had done for her mother and grandmothers.

Then, during Thanksgiving weekend of her junior year, a "blind date" arrived.

Into her life walked a teacher and mentor. David was the first person to convince her that nothing was wrong with her, even though she heard an inner voice and responded to an inner knowing.

He helped her to understand that people who JUST KNOW things are not crazy. That everyone has an inner voice and gut feelings that create an inner knowing.

Some people can hear their inner voice
and trust their inner wisdom more easily
than others.

David taught her how to go within so she
could more easily hear her inner Voice.

She discovered it is a skill that anyone can
learn. Like playing the piano or singing a
song, everyone can hear their inner voice.
For some, it is easier than others.

They are called Intuitive.

Daily she practiced all that David taught
her about going within and listening.
Slowly, she began to trust the Inner Intuitive
Voice which she had always heard inside her
head, but dared not speak about.

Once the door was open,
Liz began to meet others like her.
People also searching for
the meaning to life.

They were all LONGING
to know the answers to questions like:

"Why am I here?"

"Is there a God?"

"How do I find inner peace?"

"What is love?"

Their search took them on
journeys afar.

Some by land
Some by sea.

Some adventures took them
around the world and back again
without ever leaving their dorm!

As time went by, Liz's inner Intuitive Voice began to speak louder and louder.

She tried sharing the information she was hearing with others. A few people understood, but most just smiled uncertainly and shied away.

So instead of speaking what she heard, Liz learned to *write* what the Intuitive Voice said.

Most of the time The Voice made sense. At other times, the information about past or future events seemed so unbelievable that Liz struggled between trusting The Voice and her belief that something really was wrong with her.

One Sunday morning when summer and
graduation were drawing near,
having completed her homework,
Liz decided to have some fun by
baking a batch of Chocolate Chip Cookies.

When the cookies were in the oven, the
wonderful smell reminded her of her
grandmother and all the special times
that they had shared.

Everyday as a child, Liz would stop by
Grandma's on her way home from school.
The cookie jar was always full of Liz's
favorite Chocolate Chip Cookies
and the kitchen full of warmth and love.

That evening, filled with the glowing
memory of her grandmother and
carrying a plate overflowing with cookies,
Liz headed out across campus
to visit Marge.

Marge was now engaged to be married,
yet was depressed.

She longed for the answers to questions
like

"What is Love?"

And

"If this is Love,
why am I not at peace?"

Liz understood Marge's confusion.
She was still searching for the answers
to her own questions about love.

Unaware of just how special her gift
of inner knowing was, Liz suddenly
discovered that her Intuitive Voice
knew the answers to Marge's questions.

When she arrived at Marge's,
for the first time in a long time,
Liz found herself speaking
what her Intuitive Voice was saying.

And, as many teachers before her,
and many yet to come,
Liz's Intuitive Voice
answered Marge's questions
by telling her an analogy.

As Liz listened, she found that the analogy for Marge held answers she herself had been seeking!

"Marge," the Voice said,

"LOVE is like chocolate chip cookies. It is made up of many different ingredients.

"The key to making great cookies (or love) is KNOWING THE COMPLETE RECIPE.

"Marge, please eat one cookie and tell me
what ingredients were used to make it."

Slowly Marge ate a cookie and said,
"Flour, sugar, chocolate chips,
and butter."

"Those are some of the main ingredients,
but I doubt that if you use only
those four it would come out
as a Chocolate Chip Cookie.

"Try again,"
said the Intuitive Voice.

So, Marge ate another cookie.
This time she noticed the walnuts
and added them to her list of ingredients.

"Marge," said the Intuitive Voice,
"most adults know some of the
ingredients, but rarely is anyone
given a complete recipe for love.

"The world is changing so fast.
People are sent into the world
without a cookbook, that is,
without the rules for how to live
and how to love.

"People live in families where
 their moms and dads,
and their moms and dads,
and their moms and dads
were never taught how to
bake Chocolate Chip Cookies
(how to love).

"If you want to learn how to make
Chocolate Chip Cookies (how to love),
you have to first learn all the
ingredients and then be willing and open
to learning how to bake."

"Oh," Marge exclaimed,
"You know how I hate to cook!"

"I know," said the Intuitive Voice.

"In order to learn how to discover
the main ingredients in love, eat all the
cookies that Liz has brought you.

"Eat every one of them slowly and carefully.

"Allow yourself to receive the gift of love that Liz has given to you."

"But shouldn't Liz eat some?" Marge asked, pausing in midmunch.

"There is no need for Liz to eat any of the cookies she brought to you because she has a cookie jar full at home.

"Liz knows the recipe for Chocolate Chip Cookies so she was able to enjoy baking a batch and giving her extra cookies away.

"As Liz has done with cookies,
you can do with love.
Once you learn the recipe for love,
you will always have plenty for yourself
and enough to give to others.

**"The more love
you give away,
the more love you
will have to give."**

The Intuitive Voice went on to explain,

"There are hundreds of different recipes that will create wonderful, love-filled Chocolate Chip Cookies.

"But, you will find that they ALL have the same basic 10 ingredients.

"The portions may be different.
You may have to adjust the quantity of
the water and flour and reduce the sugar
for higher altitude.

"Some people may want
Chocolate Mint Chips, while others want
pecans instead of walnuts.
Some may not want any nuts at all,
while some little Elf may put candy
in his cookies.

"Everyone creates their own special cookie
recipe by using their unique gifts and
talents to enhance the main ingredients."

"Now that there are seven billion people
on planet Earth, there are seven billion unique
ways to create Chocolate Chip Cookies
(to know LOVE)."

The Intuitive Voice asked Marge,
"What are the main ingredients you want in
your LOVE recipe?"

Marge pondered awhile and answered,

1. Sharing the Same Interests
2. Common Goals
3. Physical Attraction
4. Great Sex
5. Good Communication
6. Trust
7. Honesty
8. Respect

"Marge," responded the Intuitive Voice, "that is great.

"What you have listed are qualities that make for a successful relationship and are the by-products of LOVE.

"However, they are NOT the
main ingredients in LOVE!"

Marge, frustrated and confused,
asked,

"Then what is love?"

The Intuitive Voice answered,

"LOVE is about connecting.

"Learning **how to connect**
and live in the 'loving'
is the journey called life.

**"You will know Love
when you feel connected . . .**

**"When you have
a sense of inner peace,
an inner knowing
that everything is okay,
that everything is perfect
just the way it is."**

The Intuitive Voice continued,

"Learning 'How to Connect'
will teach you how to
experience what love is.

"And Love, like Chocolate Chip Cookies,
has a recipe.

"I will give you one of the main ingredients.

"It is: **SLOW DOWN.**

"Stop trying to do five things at one time,
SIMPLIFY YOUR LIFE.

"Be still so that you can know that
you are a part of God.

"Stop searching outside yourself and
Go Within.

"Remember you are studying for
a Ph.D. at the University of Life.

"Be aware that sometimes the
tuition can be very expensive,
so use EVERYTHING for your
growth and advancement.

4. "Relax, and
remember to enjoy
the journey.

"Look for the 'blessing'
the goodness/Godness
in every lesson."

The evening had turned into night.
Marge and Liz were amazed
and a bit confused at what they had heard.

They spent the next few hours
reviewing what the voice had said.

Liz wanted to make sure she had
understood the message because
she realized it was also for her.

Then, since Monday's classes and final exams were calling to them, Liz gave Marge a big hug and headed back across campus.

She was still feeling confused, and she started wondering how long it would take to learn the 10 main ingredients in her recipe.

How much longer before she knew about connecting and "how to love?"

Just then the Voice began to speak again.

"Liz, you are here to teach
by awakening others.
Someday you will become a
counselor and teacher.

"But **FIRST**, you must learn how to
love 24 hours a day."

"I will be happy if I just learn what love is,"
thought Liz sourly, as she continued
along the path.

Graduation came and went.

Marge got married, found a job as a secretary, and settled into being a wife.

Even with her new life, Marge stayed in contact with Liz, and together they searched for answers, and discovered many things.

One was:

**"If You Have but One Real Friend,
You Have More Than Most."**

Eventually the path Marge took as she
searched for her recipe for Love
included divorcing.

Later, she married again and was able to
add to her recipe what she had learned
from her first time around.

This time she
created a wonderful,
loving and challenging
life filled with
two beautiful,
creative, and
gifted daughters.

Meanwhile,
Liz was offered a job in the recreation
industry. So, she headed to Colorado
to work and to search for how to know
LOVE 24 hours day.

And while she searched, Liz never forgot
the CHOCOLATE CHIP COOKIE ANALOGY
or the MOMENT the Intuitive Voice
had told her about her life purpose.

She KNEW that some day she would share
the story of Chocolate Chip Cookies with
others.

But first she had to discover her own
unique, COMPLETE recipe.

Then, like so many others,
she "Looked for Love
in All the Wrong Places."

Liz searched for Love
in the Corporate Arena,
in Business Ownership, and
in Relationships.

And she let the responsibilities of
     Life
     Work
     Home
     and
     Paying the bills
become her primary focus.

One of her teachers taught her a very important lesson.

"No matter how wise or learned someone else may be, always CHECK IT OUT.

"Ask
'IS THIS TRUTH FOR *ME?*'

"Always test the information. Go into your own kitchen and make sure the ingredient that another suggests works in your recipe."

Years passed.

It seemed to Liz that it was taking
her too long to learn what ALL
the ingredients were.

Plus, learning how to chop the nuts,
grease the pan, measure the flour,
mix all the ingredients, and how to
patiently let the cookies slowly bake
to a soft golden brown.

At times she became frustrated and weary of the journey. But, she kept searching!!

She was confident that by now
she had earned her Ph.D.
from the University of Life
with a major in the Art of Living
and a minor in Crisis Management.

She had participated in hundreds
of hours of workshops and seminars.
She had gotten a Masters Degree.

Yet, many times she still felt
empty and disconnected,
longing to experience
the answer to her original question,

"WHAT IS LOVE?"

It had been eighteen years since
the Intuitive Voice had
told Liz and Marge the
Chocolate Chip Cookie Analogy.

After all those years of saying,
"NO," she finally left her career in
the recreation industry and said
"Yes" to the message her
Intuitive Voice had given her.

Even though she felt she still did not
know her *complete recipe,* she started
using her intuition in helping/counseling
others.

The more she counseled others,
and listened to what they said,
the more she realized that there is a
"LIFE FORCE—GOD FORCE"
that is inside of everyone.

That everyone is born with a
SPIRITUAL LIFE PURPOSE.

This life purpose is what makes
everyone's recipe unique.
And it is already inside of them.

Everyone's Inner Voice already knows their own uniqueness/complete recipe. They just don't know how to get in touch with it.

Liz realized that the reason people don't hear their inner voice is because it is drowned out by their logical mind.

In addition, they do not have **FAITH** that IT may know more than their mind.

In order to discover her own
uniqueness/**Spiritual Life Purpose,**
Liz asked not a friend,
not a teacher,
not a guru,
nor a healer.

Instead, she started taking lots of
hermit time to be still and go within.
To listen to what her own Intuitive Voice
knew about her recipe for Love.

She discovered why so many others
who had tried to do the same
had lost patience and had given up.

She also learned that in order to listen
to what her Intuitive Voice
had to say about LOVE, she needed
ACCEPTANCE and GRATITUDE.

She noted those as two of the
10 main ingredients.

She realized that another ingredient
was listening to and then
**TRUSTING AND FOLLOWING
THE INTUITIVE VOICE.**
And that doing so was not always
as easy as it sounded.

Then one day she was eating
in a salad-bar restaurant,
having just passed by
Big, Soft, Chewy,
Delicious-looking
Chocolate Chip Cookies.

Liz *again* remembered the Analogy
and *again* asked her Intuitive Voice,

"WHAT IS LOVE?"

Because of all the work Liz had done to
**RELEASE HER FEARS AND CONQUER
HER ANXIETIES** and to discover
the ingredients in her recipe for
HOW TO LOVE,
this time the Voice Answered,

"Love is an always present,
always available ENERGY
that each of us can tap into at anytime,
even here in this crowded noisy restaurant.

"It is not dependent upon another person.

"You can find it
in a moment of laughter,
in the giggle of an infant,
in the glow of a sunrise or sunset,
in the flight of an eagle,
or in the miracle of a butterfly.

"LOVE IS EVERYWHERE!
LOVE IS IN EVERYTHING.

"Love is the LIFE FORCE, the essence,
the soul of all things.

"Everything is a part of God, therefore,
everyone and everything is an expression
of this LIFE FORCE.

"LOVE is the word we
use to describe a gut feeling
that we **FEEL** when
we experience the bliss
of being **CONNECTED**
to the Life Force (the Goodness,
the Godness)
in someone or something.

"When we feel connected
to another Life Force,
we say we LOVE that (fill in the blank)
situation, animal, thing . . .
or person.

"Many people feel the word love is
overused and therefore has little meaning.

"But, every time anyone says they
    LOVE
    their Spouse,
    Children,
    Pets,
    Art,
    Food,
    Motorcycle,
    Skiing,
    Football,
    the Wilderness,
    and even Chocolate Chip Cookies,

"They are describing
a sense of CONNECTION.

"LOVE IS
THE WONDERFUL EXPERIENCE
OF FEELING CONNECTED."

"One can only be fully connected to another
if they experience them right now,
in this very moment, the present!

"If one is holding any judgments or
disagreements from yesterday or has any
expectation of tomorrow, they will NOT
experience a 100% connection."

The Voice told Liz:
"Just for today don't worry about
your diet.

"Go get one of those big, soft, delicious
Chocolate Chip Cookies.

"Eat it slowly and taste every ingredient."

Trusting, she did.
And in doing so Liz actually
connected with the cookie.

She got to experience the LOVE
that comes from connecting
with the life force in ANYTHING.

ONLY THEN did she finally know
what the Voice meant when it had
told her so many years before,

"You must know how to
LOVE 24 hours a day."

As she slowly savored the
smell, taste, and texture of the
Chocolate Chip Cookie,
she remembered the night she
had walked across campus, and
The Voice had spoken to her.

Now she knew what The Voice
had meant when it told her
to learn how to experience this
wonderful sense of connecting
to all things at all times, 24/7.

Even if it meant feeling her pain
or the pain, sorrow, and anguish
of others.

Liz suddenly knew that whenever
she or her clients avoided feeling
emotional PAIN, they were limiting
themselves from fully knowing LOVE.

After all the years of learning
HOW TO LOVE/CONNECT,
Liz realized the recipe is very SIMPLE.

Unfortunately, it is not always EASY
to connect with this wonderful life force
energy that is the Goodness/Godness
in EVERYTHING.

The more she ate the cookie,
the more the inner knowing
became real.

She realized that
Only by CHOOSING
not to judge

>	pain,
>	sorrow,
>	grief,
>	hypocrisy,
>	bigotry,
>	people dying,
>	etc.

as bad or wrong, and
only by choosing
in every moment
TO ACCEPT WHAT IS,
could she connect
with this energy called Love/God,
and find INNER PEACE/LOVE.

The Intuitive Voice reminded her:

"**Happiness** is a choice,
and is experienced in the
body and mind.

"**Joy**,
is HEARTfelt
and is the result
of connecting."

As she sat and connected
to this BIG, wonderful
Chocolate Chip Cookie,
the Intuitive Voice continued.

"When you feel IN LOVE, you are not focusing on someone's imperfections.

"You feel fully connected to their Life Force, their ENERGY.

"LOVING is a blissful-JOY FULL feeling.

"Being IN LOVE is the wonderful time when you feel 100% CONNECTED to another.

"When we feel OUT OF LOVE it is because we have done something to DISCONNECT from others or they have done something to disconnect from us.

"When we feel DISCONNECTED we often try to control someone or something as a way of reconnecting.

"CONTROL is the behavior humans use instead of expressing what they are really feeling:

"FEAR.

"OR when they are feeling
one of the many subcategories of fear:

> "Anger, jealousy,
> greed, scarcity,
> abandonment,
> hopelessness,
> sadness, grief,
> low self-esteem,
> resentment,
> loss,
> or
> frustration.

"LEARNING HOW TO LOVE
is learning how to:

"Slow down,
be present,
and
CONNECT

"By accepting the person(s) or situation(s)
without any resistance or negativity.

" 'MAKING LOVE' is the most exciting and beautiful way human beings can connect.

"Sex is connecting at the physical level.

" 'Making love' is the way people connect physically, emotionally, mentally, and spiritually all at the same time.

"When a couple goes beyond having sex and actually 'make love,' they can go beyond connecting to a level where a woman bonds, and a man can fully commit.

"When such a commitment and bond occurs, the Spiritual energy (or essence) of each person is shared with the other, allowing them to 'know' each other at a deep and profound intimate level.

"The complete recipe for learning how
to love is as unique as each and every
individual."

As Liz sat in the restaurant looking back
over all the years of her journey,
she discovered that it had only been
through trial and error that
she had learned how to experience Love/
bake Chocolate Chip Cookies.

That all of life's lessons,
all the trials and errors
were what she had needed
to bring her to this very moment.

One of the major lessons
that she had learned
was she had to have
ALL the ingredients.

Liz now knew that without
all 10 ingredients,
it may have looked like
and even tasted like a cookie/love,
allowing Liz to believe that she had a
complete recipe.

But, something just wasn't right.

Over the years, when teachers and friends
whose cookie jars were overflowing
had given her one of their extra cookies,
she would eat it.

As their cookie warmed her tummy
with their love, she had heard her
Intuitive Voice say,

"When you baked, you forgot to add the
one little teaspoon of salt **(GRATITUDE)**
or baking soda **(NURTURE YOURSELF)**
or vanilla **(GIVE LOVE AWAY)**
to your cookies.

These little ingredients are very
important."

So back to the kitchen she had gone
to perfect her recipe.

And to "Check It Out."
"Are these new ingredients
Truth for me?"

Still sitting in the restaurant,
Liz realized her recipe was
the sum total of ALL the
experiences (including the people)
she had encountered throughout
her whole life.

That it was okay that it had taken her
thirty years since she first heard the
Chocolate Chip Cookie Analogy
to gain enough life experience to know

How to go within,
How to accept "What Is,"

How to be at peace
with the world as it is.

And

How to connect/love.

Liz looked at her watch and noticed that it had been only twenty minutes since she had started to eat the Chocolate Chip Cookie.

How could all that knowledge come so quickly after so many years of questioning and searching?

The Intuitive Voice began to speak again,

"It is because you have learned to
     Stop, go within,
     Look,
     Listen,
     and Trust.

"Now that you have learned
how to connect and love,
you will never need to get love
from anyone else.

"You will easily and gladly receive cookies.
And you will always know that you can bake
your own and then CONNECT with everyone
and everything by giving away your extra
cookies."

The Intuitive Voice cautioned Liz,
"Many people who are studying the art of
Chocolate Chip Cookie baking/love will want
some of your love because your recipe may
have more ingredients than theirs.

"Understand that it will be easy to give
away too many of your cookies.

"If your cookie jar becomes empty,
you may unconsciously revert to your old
way of filling your cookie jar by getting
cookies/love from someone else.

"If your cookie jar becomes empty—
and it may in your process
of understanding about love—
find someone whose cookie jar is
overflowing and spend time in their
presence.

"Just the smell of their cookie jar
can awaken the memory of the recipe
inside of you.

OR

"Go into nature and ask Mother Earth
to whisper the recipe in your ear.

"Walk along the beach and then sit and
watch as the waves splash the ingredient
list upon the shore.

"Listen to music and connect with the universal language of all beings.

"Draw a picture,
play in the sandbox,
get dirty.

"Watch a child who has
not yet learned to judge.

"THEN

"STOP,
LOOK,
and
LISTEN!

"STOP—
right now, slow down
and Go Within and connect
to your inner Intuitive Voice.

"LOOK—
around you and notice
whether you are trusting

"Or are you:

"Complaining about the past?
worrying about the future?
judging yourself or another?
playing the victim or the martyr?

"LISTEN—
to your gut feelings.
They will guide you,
for they are an aspect
of your Intuitive Voice.

"INTUITION IS THE WAY
GOD SPEAKS TO US.

"Listen and you will be guided!

When you have discovered your own special way of how to connect and how to keep your cookie jar full, you will always be able to bake extra cookies and **give them (love) away.**

"Especially to all the people who are still needing to learn the ingredients that it takes to know how to connect/love."

Liz was glowing with the wonderful
sense of calm and inner peace that
she had longed for.

With that, Liz sensed a smile from her
Intuitive Voice as it reminded her that,

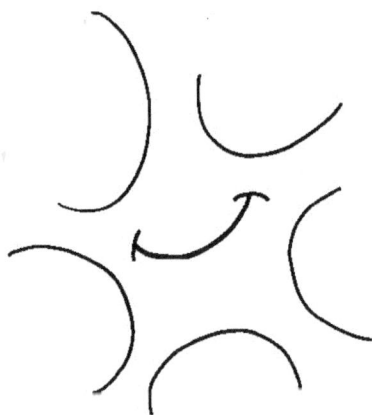

"Love is about connection.
Learning how to connect
and live in the 'loving'
is the journey called life.

"You will know love
when you feel connected

"When you have a sense of inner peace;
an inner knowing that everything is okay,
that everything is perfect
just the way it is.

"It is just an illusion
that anyone is
ever disconnected.

"LOVE IS
THE WONDERFUL EXPERIENCE
OF FEELING CONNECTED.

"The key is learning the recipe for love and all the ingredients so you can live more fully in the connection."

Recipe for CONNECTION

1. Slow Down—Simplify Your Life
2. Release Your Fears and Conquer Your Anxieties
3. Accept What is
4. Forgive
5. Have Faith in God
6. Trust and Follow Your Intuition
7. Be Grateful
8. Nurture Yourself
9. Give Love Away
10. Discover Your Spiritual Life Purpose— Your Uniqueness.

You are here for a reason,
    You have been given a season
        to experience LOVE.
It is not about what you are
        here To DO,
It is about what you are here
        To BE.

The End

In order to learn more about "how to connect" look for Nancy R. Harris' **second book RX For Loving - Holistic Prescription For Creating Spiritual Connections**. It expands upon all the ingredients and shares delightful and touching true stories of Nancy's own and other people's journey.

Each chapter provides suggestions and how-to's that you can easily incorporate into your life. These suggestions will assist you in discovering your own unique recipe for love/connection.

In addition, it walks you through the unique technique Nancy uses with her clients that has allowed every one of them to discover their innate Spiritual Life Purpose.

Unique Chocolate Chip Cookie Recipes

Everyone can enjoy Chocolate Chip Cookies, even if they are on a special diet and must avoid sugar, fat, lactose, eggs, wheat, or gluten.

Remember, always keep your cookie jar full with your own unique recipe. How will you individualize your recipe? Will you add walnuts, pecans, almonds, or macadamia nuts? Will you choose mint chips, peanut butter, or cherry chips as a variation?

Nancy's grandma's cookie jar always welcomed her with big, chewy, soft, love-filled Chocolate Chip Cookies. Now she enjoys Carol Fenster's Wheat-Free, Gluten-Free cookies and gives dieting friends cookies made from the *Vegetarian Times Complete Cookbook's* recipe that is fat free and sugar free.

Three unique cookie recipes have been included so you can easily "connect" by giving those you love the gift of homemade Chocolate Chip Cookies when you give them a copy of this book. (#9 Give Love Away)

Nancy's Favorite Recipe For Chocolate Chip Cookies

1   cup butter, margarine (stick), or shortening
3/4 cup granulated (white) sugar
3/4 cup brown sugar
  2 large eggs
  2 teaspoons vanilla

2 1/4 cups all-purpose flour
  1 teaspoon baking soda
  1 teaspoon salt
  2 cups chocolate chips or a combination of chocolate
      chips and other flavors of chips (white chocolate,
      mint, cherry, peanut butter, butterscotch, etc.)
  1 cup chopped pecans, walnuts, almonds, macadamia nuts,
      or a mixture (optional)

Be creative! Express your uniqueness!
Create a cookie that expresses you and the
depth of love you want to share!

Directions:
Preheat oven to 350 degrees F (175 degrees C). Lightly
grease cookie sheets. (Too much grease will cause cookies to
spread and become too thin and/or burn. Some people prefer
to use an ungreased or nonstick cookie sheet. For best
results, cook with only one cookie sheet in the oven. Cool
cookie sheet between batches or have second one ready.)

In a large bowl, cream the butter, margarine or shortening, together with the brown sugar and white sugar until light and fluffy. (Use electric mixer if available.)

Add the eggs one at a time, beating well each time you add an egg. Then add the vanilla.

Fold in the chocolate chips and/or other flavor chips and your choice of nuts. (Nuts optional)

Drop by rounded tablespoon onto prepared cookie sheet.

Bake for 8 to 12 minutes until light brown. Time will vary depending on oven, size of cookies, and altitude.

Immediately remove cookies and let cool on wire rack.

ENJOY!!!

High Altitude: Remember to adjust recipe by increasing the flour by 1/4 cup and adding 2 teaspoons of water.

Wheat-Free, Gluten-Free Chocolate Chip Cookies

1/4   cup butter or margarine (softened, not melted)
3/4   cup brown sugar
1/3   cup granulated sugar
  2   teaspoon vanilla extract
  1   extra large egg (or egg substitute)
3/4   cup brown rice flour or grabanzo/fava bean flour
1/2   cup tapioca flour
1/4   cup potato starch
1/2   teaspoon baking soda
  1   teaspoon xanthan gum
1/4   teaspoon salt
1 1/2 cup gluten-free chocolate chips

Preheat oven to 350 degrees. In large mixing bowl, use electric mixer to beat butter (or margarine), brown and white sugars, and vanilla extract together until smooth. Beat in egg. In separate bowl, whisk together flours, xanthan gum, and salt. Beat into egg mixture on low speed until incorporated. Dough will be somewhat stiff. Stir in chocolate chips.

Drop by tablespoons (or use a small spring-action ice cream scoop for evenly sized cookies) onto nonstick cookie sheet lined with parchment paper or nonstick liner sprayed with cooking spray.

Bake for 10-12 minutes or until cookies are lightly puffed and slightly brown. Cool on rack. Store in airtight container. Makes 24.

Reprinted with permission from Carol Fenster, Ph.D. Savory Palate Press. To learn more about cooking without wheat, gluten, dairy, egg, yeast, and sugar, go to www.savorypalate.com

NO FAT - NO SUGAR
Chocolate Chip Taste-Alikes

Typical chocolate chip cookies are high in fat, sugar, and calories. Not these taste-alikes. They contain almost no fat*, are sweetened with honey instead of sugar, and have only 55 calories per cookie.

- 3 cups whole-wheat flour
- 1 teaspoon baking soda
- 3/4 cup unsweetened applesauce
- 3/4 cup honey
- 2 teaspoon vanilla extract
- 3/4 cup unsweetened carob chips or semisweet chocolate chips
- 1/2 cup chopped nuts or sunflower seeds (optional)

PREHEAT the oven to 350 degrees. In a large bowl, combine the flour and baking soda. Stir together the applesauce, honey, and vanilla in a separate bowl. Add the dry ingredients and stir well. Fold in the carob chips or chocolate chips and nuts.

DROP the batter by the tablespoonfuls onto a nonstick or lightly oiled cookie sheet. Flatten with a fork.

BAKE until light brown, about 12 minutes.

*With nuts only .9 g fat per cookie.

Recipe reprinted with permission from *Vegetarian Times Complete Cookbook* by the Editors of *Vegetarian Times*. Copyright 1995, Vegetarian Times, Inc.

About the Author

Dr. Nancy R. Harris, DSS is a Professional Intuitive and Psychotherapist with 54 years of experience using her intuitive and empathic gifts and has over 40 years of study in spiritual and metaphysical methodologies.

Dr. Harris specializes in Spiritual Psychology and Energy Psychology. Based on 25 years of study in Energy Psychology, Dr. Harris has created a powerful technique called Quick and Easy Emotional Release™ (QEER™). Her technique draws from 6 different modalities and her own intuitive abilities.

Dr. Harris is internationally known for her unique and transformational training programs and private intuitive counseling. Her most popular training program is the highly successful and spiritually transformational Intuitive Awareness Training™.

About the Author

Many of Dr. Harris' clients go beyond just finding answers. They also discover a greater sense of connection and realize their innate spiritual life purpose. She has shared her wisdom with over 1000 people as clients and workshop participants.

Dr. Harris had her own Spiritual awakening in 1958 when she was nine years old and has been on her journey ever since. Since leaving home at seventeen, she has traveled the world and has studied with many masters. She has a Bachelor's Degree in Sociology and a Master's and Doctorate in Spiritual Science.

Nancy lives and skis in Colorado. She is available for workshops and private sessions upon request. Her life is dedicated to "Awaking people to their Intuitive Voice" and to personal transformation.

She hopes this book has awakened within you the desire to enrich your life by CONNECTING!

Notes

Notes

www.ingramcontent.com/pod-product-compliance
Lightning Source LLC
Chambersburg PA
CBHW071601040426
42452CB00008B/1254